TRAVEL GUIDE TO THE UNITED STATES

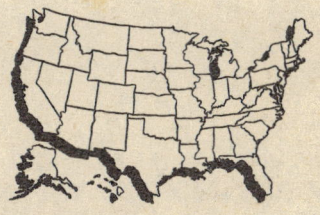

Volume Three:
North Dakota to Wyoming

by
Jack Spencer

SANTA MONICA PRESS
P.O. Box 1076
Santa Monica, CA 90406-1076
Printed in the United States
All Rights Reserved

This book may not be reproduced
in whole or in part or in any
form or format without written
permission of the publisher

©1994 SANTA MONICA PRESS

TABLE OF CONTENTS

North Dakota	5
Ohio	11
Oklahoma	19
Oregon	25
Pennsylvania	31
Rhode Island	41
South Carolina	47
South Dakota	53
Tennesse	59
Texas	67
Utah	77
Vermont	83
Virginia	87
Washington	97
Washington, D.C.	105
West Virginia	113
Wisconsin	119
Wyoming	125

TRAVEL GUIDE TO THE UNITED STATES

AN IMPORTANT NOTE

When planning your vacation, you should always phone the attractions that you would like to visit. While the material in this book has been completed with the most up-to-date information available, some attractions change their prices and hours of operation without warning, some are forced to close due to unpredictable weather, and some — many national parks, for instance — require advance reservations.

TRAVEL GUIDE TO THE UNITED STATES

NORTH DAKOTA

Attractions

Hatten-Eielson Museum
Open year-round, every day. Located in Hatton. This museum honors Carl Ben Eielson, one of America's earliest and foremost aviators. There are many antiques housed in this one hundred year old house.

State Capitol Building
Open year-round, 9 a.m. to 4 p.m. Saturday, 1 p.m. to 4 p.m. Sunday (8 a.m. to 4 p.m. Monday to Friday, from Memorial Day to Labor Day). Located on North 6th Street in Bismarck. Call (701) 224-2480. Free. This capitol building is a stunning high-rise, containing a museum and towering almost 20 stories high.

Historic Sites and Monuments

Double Ditch Indian Village
State Historic Site
Open year-round, every day. Located on Route 1804, about 10 miles north of Bismarck. Visit the remains of a Mandan Native American village that was active during the 1700s. Features the remains of houses and strongholds.

Fort Clark Historic Site
Open year-round, 9 a.m. to 5 p.m. daily (9 a.m. to 10 p.m. from May to August). Located about 10 miles south of Stanton. Tour one of the famous fur trading posts from the early 19th century.

Fort Totten State Historic Site
Open from June to October, 8 a.m. to 6 p.m. daily. Located on Route 57, several miles south of Devils Lake. Free. Tour one of the most important US Army forts in the area. It was active in the late 19th century.

Fort Union Trading Post National Historic Site
Open year-round, 9 a.m. to 5:30 p.m. daily (8 a.m. to 8 p.m. daily during the summer months). Located about 30 miles south of Williston on Route 1804. Call (701) 572-9083. Free. This site features the restored fur trading post that was crucial to the industry of the area for almost 40 years.

Geographical Center Historical Society
Open year-round, every day. Located in Rugby. Visit the geographical center of North America. This site features a beautifully restored village from the pioneer days, with over 25 complete buildings.

TRAVEL GUIDE TO THE UNITED STATES

Knife River Indian Villages National Historic Site

Open year-round, 8 a.m. to 4:30 p.m. daily (8 a.m. to 8 p.m. during summer months). Located north of Stanton on Route 31. Call (701) 745-3300. Free. This site features the ruins of several villages of the Plains Native Americans. Features many cultural presentations and exhibits.

Pembina State Historical Site and Museum

Open from Memorial Day to Labor Day, 10 a.m. to 5 p.m. weekdays. Located in Pembina State Park in Pembina. Free. This museum features many displays about the history of the area, including everything from Native American arts and crafts to items from World War II.

Whitestone Hill Battlefield State Historic Site

Open from May to September, 8 a.m. to 8 p.m. daily. Located on Route 281, north of Ellendale. Free. Visit the field where one of the fiercest battles between Native Americans and US Army troops took place. The battle lasted three days.

National Parks and Recreation Areas

International Peace Garden

Open year-round, every day, but cold weather often forces closure during the winter months. Located on Route 281, just north of Dunseith. Call (701) 263-4390. There is an admission charge of $2 for each individual or $5 for each vehicle, and you can buy a yearly entrance for $10; there is a charge of up to $10 for camping. This beautiful garden symbolizes the peaceful coexistence of the United States of America and Canada. Its picturesque scenery and landscaping make it perfect for picnics or walks. There are bell towers, amphitheaters, chapels, auditoriums, and a host of other interesting sites to see. There is camping, but there are no cabins or lodges. You can even eat at one of several restaurants.

Theodore Roosevelt National Park

Open year-round, every day, but sudden extremes in weather can cause closure unexpectedly. Located off of Interstate 94 in Medora. Call (701) 623-4466. There is a $3 charge for admission and a $7 charge for camping. Situated along the Little Missouri River, this national park contains the sites of some of Roosevelt's ranches. Perfect for horseback riding, hiking, camping, and cross-country skiing; it is quite likely that you will come across a herd of buffalo. There are many miles of hiking trails, well suited to all levels of experience, and there are quite a few campsites, but there are no cabins or lodges. You can hike and camp in the backcountry.

Amusement Parks

Lucy's Amusement Park
Open year-round, 10 a.m. to 10 p.m. daily. Located on Highway 83 South in Minot. Call (701) 839-2320. There is a charge for each ride. If you're looking for a place to take your small kids, then Lucy's Amusement Park is just the spot for you. It features over half a dozen rides designed especially for small children, one of which is a great slide. Your older children can ride around in go-karts, and you can all play a game of mini-golf.

TRAVEL GUIDE TO THE UNITED STATES

OHIO

Attractions

Garst Museum
Open from February to December, 1 p.m. to 4:30 p.m. Tuesday to Sunday. Located at 205 North Broadway in Gnadenhutten. Free. This museum features many exhibits chronicling the history of the region, including items remaining from the Indian War period.

Harding Museum
Open year-round, every day. Located at 380 Mount Vernon Avenue in Marion. Tour the one hundred year old house in which Warren G. Harding lived. The porch where he presented many of his presidential campaign speeches still stands today. The house contains many of his personal belongings.

Neil Armstrong Air and Space Museum
Open from March to November, every day. Located off of Interstate 75 in Wapakoneta. Call (419) 738-8811. There is an entry fee. This fascinating museum not only commemorates Neil Armstrong, the first man to walk on the moon, but it also covers the history of space flight. A thoroughly entertaining place that the whole family will love!

Pro Football Hall of Fame
Open year-round, every day. Located at 2121 Harrison Avenue North West in Canton. Tour the hall of fame of one of the most popular sports in the country. Features hundreds of exhibits about great games and athletes.

State Capitol Building
Open year-round, 8 a.m. to 5 p.m. Monday to Friday, 9 a.m. to 5 p.m. weekends. Located on High Street in Columbus. Call (614) 466-2125. Free. Tour the beautiful capitol building of Ohio. Many historical exhibits are contained within.

Statue of Abraham Lincoln
Open year-round, dawn to dusk daily. Located at 421 East 4th Street in Cincinnati. Free. This statue, sculpted by George Grey Barnard, is widely considered to be one of the finest in the country.

Toledo Museum of Art
Open year-round, 9 a.m. to 5 p.m. Tuesday to Saturday, 1 p.m. to 5 p.m. Sunday. Located at 2445 Monroe Street in Toledo. Call (419) 255-8000. Free. This fine museum features displays on everything from classical civilizations to modern American art. Considered one of the best art museums in the world.

United States Air Force Museum
Open year-round, 9 a.m. to 5 p.m. weekdays, 10 a.m. to 6 p.m. weekends. Located at Wright-Patterson Air Force Base in Dayton. Call (513) 255-3284. Free. This terrific museum lets you get close to hundreds of exhibits, photos, and airplanes, including a section devoted to Prisoners of War.

Historic Sites and Monuments

Adena State Memorial
Open year-round, every day. Located on Adena Road in Chillicothe. Tour the two hundred-year old house of the first senator of Ohio. Features many beautiful antiques.

James A. Garfield National Historic Site
Open year-round, noon to 5 p.m. Sunday, 10 a.m. to 5 p.m. Tuesday to Saturday. Located at 8095 Mentor Avenue in Mentor. Call (216) 255-8722. There is a reasonable charge for admission. Tour the house and grounds of James A Garfield. This estate is also known as Lawnfield.

Leo Petroglyphs
Open year-round, dawn to dusk daily. Located just outside of Coalton. Free. These Native

American petroglyphs are truly fascinating to observe. They are evidence of civilized cultures dating back thousands of years.

Mound City Group National Monument
Open year-round, 8 a.m. to 5 p.m. daily (8 a.m. to 7 p.m. daily from June to Labor Day). Located at 16062 State Route 104 in Chillicothe. Call (614) 774-1125. There is a reasonable charge for admission. This monument commemorates the Hopewell Native American tribe that populated this region approximately 2 millennia ago. Archaeologists have discovered some incredible art in these huge burial mounds.

Seip Mound State Memorial
Open year-round, dawn to dusk daily. Located on Route 50, just east of Bainbridge. Free. Visit this awe-inspiring Native American burial ground and watch archaeological excavations.

William Howard Taft
National Historic Site
Open year-round, 10 a.m. to 4 p.m. daily. Located at 2038 Auburn Avenue in Cincinnati. Call (513) 684-3262. Free. Tour the house where Chief Justice and President William Howard Taft spent his childhood. Features presentations and exhibits.

Wright Brothers Memorial

Open year-round, dawn to dusk daily. Located near Wright Field in Dayton. Free. This memorial commemorates the outstanding achievements of Orville and Wilbur Wright, the two pioneers of aviation.

National Parks and Recreation Areas

Cuyahoga Valley
National Recreation Area

Open year-round, 8 a.m. to 11 p.m. daily, but inclement weather forces closure of certain areas during the winter. Located at 15610 Baughn Road in Brecksville. Call (216) 650-4636. This beautiful valley is perfect for horseback riding, cycling, fishing, swimming, picnicking, and hiking during the summer, and great for skiing (cross-country and alpine), skating, and sledding during the winter. There are miles and miles of hiking trails within the recreation area, suited for people at all levels of experience. There are plenty of performances and presentations for you to watch, including reenactments of historic life in a rural village, musicals and plays in amphitheaters, and antique trains. There is even a professional-quality golf course.

Amusement Parks

Cedar Point

Open from May to September, 9 a.m. to 10 p.m. daily. Located off of Route 250 in Sandusky. Call (419) 626-0830. There is an admission charge of about $25, and there is an additional charge for parking. You can buy a ticket for the following day for $10 more. This is the biggest amusement park in the entire country — over 350 acres! It has almost 60 rides, 10 of which are roller coasters! The landscaping is very natural, so expect to do plenty of walking through trails in the woods. Since the park is on the shore of Lake Erie, you can approach it by boat (the swimming is great!). Some of the more popular rides include the highest roller coaster in the world, a huge Ferris wheel, and a log ride. There are plenty of shows for you to see, including IMAX movies and musical theater. You can eat at almost 50 different places, serving everything from sandwiches to full meals. Most people stay at this park for more than one day.

Kings Island

Open from April to October, 9 a.m. to 11 p.m. daily. Located at Kings Island Drive in Kings Island. Call (513) 398-5600. There is an admission charge of about $25, and an additional charge for parking. You can buy a ticket for the following day for under $10. This is one of the biggest and best amusement parks in the country — almost three hundred acres! It features 52 water and land rides, about one-fourth of which are designed specifically for younger kids. Some of the more popular rides include the longest roller coaster in the country, a raft ride, and a flight simulator. There are plenty of performances for you to see, such as illusionists, musicals, and trained animals. And you might even bump into a Smurf! You can take a monorail ride through the Wild Animal Habitat, the park's famous wild animal safari.

Sea World of Ohio

Open from May to September, 9 a.m. to 11 p.m.. Located at 1100 Sea World Drive in Aurora. Call (216) 995-2121. There is an admission charge of about $20, but there is no charge for parking. Like the other Sea World parks, this one doesn't feature any mechanical rides, but it is a wonderful way to introduce your family to the mysteries of nature. The informative and entertaining shows will teach you about many different aquatic creatures, such as sea lions, seals, and killer whales. Your kids can even participate in some of the shows and feed the animals. There are also several exciting water sport shows. You can grab a bite to eat at almost 20 different locations.

TRAVEL GUIDE TO THE UNITED STATES

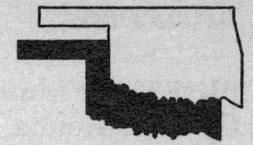

OKLAHOMA

TRAVEL GUIDE TO THE UNITED STATES

Attractions

Black Kettle Museum
Open year-round, 9 a.m. to 5 p.m. Monday to Saturday, 1 p.m. to 5 p.m. Sunday. Located on Route 283 in Cheyenne. Call (405) 497-3929. Free. This museum chronicles one of General Custer's attacks on a Native American tribe.

Chickasaw Council House
Open year-round, 9 a.m. to 5 p.m. Tuesday to Friday, 2 p.m. to 5 p.m. weekends. Located in Tishomingo. Free. This tiny, 140 year old log house was the first capitol building of the Indian Territory. A museum displays various arts and crafts of the Chickasaw Native Americans.

Creek National Capitol
Open year-round, 9 a.m. to 5 p.m. Tuesday to Saturday. Located at 112 West 6th Street in Okmulgee. Call (918) 756-2324. Free. This museum features many exhibits highlighting the beauty of the Creek Native American tribe's culture. There are also several presentations.

Frank Phillips Home
Open year-round, 9 a.m. to 5 p.m. Tuesday to Friday, 2 p.m. to 5 p.m. Saturday and Sunday. Located at 1107 South East Cherokee Avenue in

Bartlesville. Call (918) 336-2491. Free. Tour the beautiful mansion of Frank Phillips, one of the first oil tycoons in Oklahoma. Features many antiques and personal belongings.

Marland Mansion
Open year-round, every day. Located on Monument Road in Ponca City. Tour the beautiful mansion of E.W. Marland, one of Oklahoma's oil tycoons. Features many antiques and personal belongings.

Philomathic Museum
Open year-round, 1 p.m. to 5 p.m. Monday to Saturday. Located at 311 East Main Street in Andarko. Free. This museum features many interesting exhibits about the history of the region, including army uniforms, Native American crafts, and antique trains.

Price Tower
Open year-round, every day. Located on Dewey Avenue in Bartlesville. This skyscraper, penned by architect Frank Lloyd Wright, is considered one of the finest examples of modern architecture in the world.

Sod House Museum
Open year-round, 9 a.m. to 5 p.m. Tuesday to Friday, 2 p.m. to 5 p.m. weekends. Located on

Highway 8 outside of Aline. This sod house dates all the way back to the first pioneers of the state! Museum exhibits include antique farm equipment.

State Capitol Building
Open year-round, 8 a.m. to 5 p.m. weekdays, 8 a.m. to 4 p.m. weekends. Located at Lincoln Boulevard in Oklahoma City. Call (405) 521-3356. Admission is free, but there is a charge for a tour. This beautifully ornate building has many marble features and contains histories of the area.

Tom Mix Museum
Open year-round, 9 a.m. to 5 p.m. Tuesday to Friday, and 1 p.m. to 5 p.m. weekends. Located on Don Tyler Avenue in Dewey. Free. This museum commemorates the famous cowboy Tom Mix. Many exhibits, including an old-fashioned nickelodeon in which you can watch his movies.

Historic Sites and Monuments

Lynn Riggs Memorial
Open from September to June, 8 a.m. to 4:30 p.m. weekdays, 1:30 p.m. to 4:30 p.m. weekends. Call (918) 341-7510, extension 264. Lynn

Riggs is one of the most celebrated writers in Oklahoma's history. She wrote the book upon which the play *Oklahoma!* was based. You can see many of her belongings, including first drafts of her works.

Veterans of Foreign Wars Memorial
Open year-round, dawn to dusk daily. Located in the City Park in Bristow. Free. Visit one of the most famous memorials in the United States commemorating those who fought to defend her. There is a museum with many fascinating items and displays.

Will Rogers Memorial
Open year-round, 8 a.m. to 5 p.m. daily. Located on Route 88, just west of Claremore. Call (918) 341-0719. Free. This memorial features a beautiful ranch and grounds that commemorate the American satirist. A well-known statue of Will Rogers is on permanent display.

National Parks and Recreation Areas

Chickasaw National Recreation Area
Open year-round, every day, but severe weather conditions (such as tornadoes) are common in the spring and summer. Located on

Route 7 near Sulphur. Call (405) 622-3161. There is a charge of $6 for camping, collected nightly. This recreation area features beautiful terrain: hilly forests, lakes, wells, and springs. Perfect for boating, swimming, camping, hiking, and cycling, the temperature is quite moderate year-round. There are miles of hiking trails suited to all levels of experience, and there are plenty of campsites, but there are no cabins or lodges.

Amusement Parks

Frontier City
Open from April to September, 5 p.m. to 10 p.m. Tuesday to Friday, and noon to 10 p.m. Saturday and Sunday. Located at 11601 Northeast Expressway in Oklahoma City. Call (405) 478-2414. There is an admission charge of around $15, and an additional charge for parking. This park lets you experience the Old West. Yeeeeeehaaaawww, Pardner! It features several rides, some of which are designed specifically for younger children, but a lot of the fun comes just from the atmosphere. Some of the more popular rides include a log ride and several roller coasters. You can also play carnival games and video games. There are many presentations put on each day, such as a gunfight, an illusionist, and fireworks.

TRAVEL GUIDE TO THE UNITED STATES

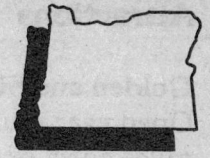

OREGON

Attractions

Golden and Silver Falls State Park
Open year-round, every day. Located about 25 miles north of Coos Bay. Free on weekdays. Watch these two picturesque and mammoth waterfalls.

Pittock Mansion
Open year-round, 9 a.m. to 5 p.m. daily. Located at 3229 North West Pittock Drive in Portland. Call (503) 248-4469. There is an admission fee of $6. This beautiful European style manor sits atop the hills to the north of the city. The view is incredible, and the house is filled with some of the finest art in the country.

Portland Art Museum
Open year-round, 9 a.m. to 5 p.m. Tuesday to Sunday. Located at 1219 South West Park Avenue in Portland. Call (503) 226-2811. There is an admission fee of about $5. One of the finest art museums in the west, this facility features art from around the world dating back almost four thousand years!

Powell's City of Books
Open year-round, 9 a.m. to 5 p.m. daily. Located at 1005 West Burnside Street in Portland. Call (503) 228-4651. If you're a bookworm (and

you must be, considering you're reading this right now), then you won't want to miss Powell's. This book store is so huge, that it might actually be the biggest in the world.

Undersea Gardens
Open year-round, 9 a.m. to 5 p.m. daily. Located at 250 South West Bay Boulevard in Newport. Call (503) 256-2206. There is an admission fee of about $5. If you've ever wanted to know what it's like to live under the sea, then prepare to find out. This popular tourist site lets you look into the bottom of the bay from a special viewing area.

Historic Sites and Monuments

Astoria Column
Open year-round, 8 a.m. to sunset daily. Located on Coxcomb Hill in Astor. Free. This tower was created in honor of the founding of Astoria. The magnificent view from the top looks out over the Columbia River.

Fort Clatsop National Memorial
Open year-round, 8 a.m. to 5 p.m. (8 a.m. to 6 p.m. during summer months). Located on Route 101, about 5 miles outside of Astoria. Call (503) 861-2471. $1 entry fee per person from

April to September, but free the rest of the year. This memorial is where the explorers Lewis and Clark camped over the winter of 1805-6 during their expedition. Features beautiful trails and informative presentations.

John Day Fossil Beds National Monument
Open year-round, every day, but Monument Headquarters is only open during business hours on weekdays. Headquarters located at 420 West Main Street in John Day (they can provide directions to the various units which make up the monument). Call (503) 575-0721. Free. This monument has fossils of animals and plants from four geological periods. Beautiful scenery and trails, along with fossil presentations.

McLoughlin House National Historic Site
Open year-round except January, 10 a.m. to 4 p.m. Tuesday to Saturday, and 1 p.m. to 4 p.m. Sunday. Located in McLoughlin Park just east of Highway 99, in Oregon City. Call (503) 656-5146. $2.50 per adult, $2 per senior, and $1 per child over 6. This site is the pioneer home of John McLoughlin, one of Oregon's founding fathers. The house predates Oregon's entry into the United States of America.

Oregon Historical Center

Open year-round, 10 a.m. to 4:45 p.m. Monday to Saturday. Located at 1230 South West Park Avenue in Portland. Call (503) 222-1741. Free. This museum has entertaining exhibits to tell you everything you could want to know about the region, from pioneers to Native American art.

Oregon Trail Marker

Open year-round. Located at Laurel Hill on Route 26. Free. This site marks the perilous route taken by pioneers on this famous trail.

National Parks and Recreation Areas

Crater Lake National Park

Open year-round, 8 a.m. to dusk daily. Located on Route 62 in Crater Lake. Call (503) 594-2211. There is an admission charge of $5, and an additional charge of $10 for camping. One of the most beautiful National Parks in the country, it features a huge lake that was once the crater of a volcano. The lake is perfect for fishing and boating, and there are hundreds of miles of hiking trails that lead up to it (well suited to all levels of experience). You can also find many beautiful spots to have a picnic, and you can camp at one of many designated areas. If you are more daring, you can even venture out into the backcountry. Remember to bring a shovel and other snow equipment, as there is *heavy* snowfall. If you prefer to camp in a bit more comfort, then there are lodges in which you can stay (don't forget to make a reservation).

Amusement Parks

Oaks Park
Open from March to October, 1 p.m. to 10 p.m. Tuesday to Friday, and noon to 10 p.m. Saturday and Sunday. Located on Southeast Oaks Parkway in Portland. Call (503) 233-5777. Admission is free, but there is a charge for each ride. Parking is free. This mid-sized fun park has 25 rides nestled among its many oak trees. Some of these rides include several roller coasters, a haunted mine, a Ferris wheel, and scooters. Several of the attractions are contained within buildings dating back to the early 1900s. There is also a mini-golf course, and children's theatre companies and bands often perform in the park (especially over the summer months). There are several fast food stands, but you can bring your own food with you.

TRAVEL GUIDE TO THE UNITED STATES

PENNSYLVANIA

Attractions

Betsy Ross' House
Open year-round, Monday to Saturday. Located at 239 Arch Street in Philadelphia. Call (215) 627-5343. Philadelphia is one of the most historic towns in the country, and this is one of the most historic places in the town. This is the real house where the first American flag was sewn! A really fun place to visit.

The Carnegie
Open year-round, every day. Located at 4400 Forbes Avenue in Pittsburgh. Call (412) 622-3313. One of the finest cultural centers in the world, this attraction is virtually a one-stop institute where you can experience art and literature. It features a Music Hall, the Carnegie Library, a Museum of Natural History, and a Museum of Art. A must-see!

Chadds Ford Inn
Located at Routes 1 and 100, Chadds Ford, Pennsylvania. Call (215) 388-7361. This historic 18th century restaurant has hosted such great American figures as Martha Washington, who stopped in for a meal while she was on her to way to meet her husband at Valley Forge. Situated in Andrew Wyeth country, the lovely inn features the artist's work on its walls.

Classic American dishes are served in a warm setting that defines Americana.

City Hall
Open year-round, 9 a.m. to 5 p.m. weekdays. Located on Broad Street in Philadelphia. Call (215) 567-4476. Free. One of the oldest buildings in Pennsylvania, this is a masterpiece of structure! Featuring elaborate accents and fine masonry, there is a statue of William Penn, the founder of the state, on the roof. This was when they really knew how to make buildings!

Governor's Home
Open from May to October, 10 a.m. to 2 p.m. Tuesday and Thursday. Located at 2035 North Front Street in Harrisburg. Free. Although this mansion was built fairly recently, it has all the elegance and grandeur of the oldest buildings in the state. Moreover, it features many beautiful antiques and valuable works of art.

Independence Hall
Open year-round, every day. Located on Chestnut Street in Philadelphia (in Independence Square). Call (215) 597-8974. Free. One of the most important buildings in the country; the Declaration of Independence was drafted and signed here! The Articles of Confederation and the Constitution were also ratified within these

chambers. The building also served as one of the first houses of Congress. A tour here will truly bring American history to life. Incidentally, you don't want to leave without first visiting the Liberty Bell, also in Independence Square.

Railroad Museum of Pennsylvania
Open year-round, every day. Located on Route 741 in Strasburg. Call (717) 687-8628. There is a $5 charge for admission. This country couldn't have expanded to the size it is today if it hadn't been for the railroad, and this exciting museum explores the contributions that this form of transportation has made to history. The trains on display are really neat, and a visit here will be enjoyed by the whole family.

Robert E. Lee Headquarters and Museum
Open from March to November, 9 a.m. to 5 p.m. daily (until 9 p.m. from April to October). Located at 401 Buford Avenue in Franklin Center. Call (717) 334-3141. Free. This fascinating museum is a must-see for military history buffs! Not only does it features displays and exhibits on famous Civil War battles, such as Gettysburg, but is also has Union and Confederate uniforms on display.

Historic Sites and Monuments

**Alleghany Portage Railroad
National Historic Site**
Open year-round, 8:30 a.m. to 5 p.m. daily. Located off of Highway 22 in Cresson. Call (814) 886-8176. Free. The railroad has been one of the most important modes of transportation in America, allowing people and items to travel economically over vast distances. This historic site commemorates the train line that crossed the Allegheny Mountains. Many of the old buildings along the line are still intact, and performers in period clothing act out the duties of railroad workers. A wonderful place to visit.

Benjamin Franklin National Memorial
Open year-round, 10 a.m. to 4:30 p.m. daily. Located on 20th Street in Philadelphia. Call (215) 448-1329. Free. This statue commemorates the life of Benjamin Franklin, whose achievements ranged from conducting scientific experiments to being the U.S. ambassador to France. You can also visit the Franklin Institute Science museum, one of the finest and most advanced science museums in the country. There is an admission charge of $12.50 to the museum, which is well worth the price. A really great place to spend the afternoon.

Edgar Allen Poe National Historic Site
Open year-round, 9 a.m. to 5 p.m. daily. Located on 7th Street in Philadelphia. Call (215) 597-8780. Free. This is the beautiful urban home of famed horror writer Edgar Allen Poe. You can tour the house and participate in several programs which celebrate the author's works.

Eisenhower National Historic Site
Open from April to October, 9 a.m. to 4 p.m. daily, and from November to March, 9 a.m. to 4 p.m. Wednesday to Sunday. Located on Route 134 in Gettysburg. Call (717) 334-1124. Dwight D. Eisenhower, one of the most popular presidents of all time, spent his golden years with his wife on this beautiful farm. You can tour the house in which the two lived.

Fort Necessity National Battlefield
Open year-round, 10:30 a.m. to 5 p.m. daily. Located on Route 40 in Farmington. Call (412) 329-5512. There is an admission charge of $1 for each adult. This site perfectly captures the spirit of colonial times by preserving an old cemetery, a pub that was popular with colonial soldiers, and several battlegrounds where troops under 22 year old George Washington fought in the French and Indian War. There are plenty of presentations and displays to entertain you.

National Parks and Recreation Areas

Gettysburg National Military Park
Open year-round, 9 a.m. to 5 p.m. daily. Located on Taneytown Road in Gettysburg. Call (717) 334-1124. There is an admission charge of $2 for each adult and $1 for each child, and an additional charge of $20 if you want a guided tour. The site of the most famous and most important battle of the Civil War, Gettysburg made the Union victory inevitable. President Lincoln spoke aloud the words of his famous Gettysburg Address ("Four score and seven years ago...") here for the first time, in honor of the men who died in the battle. This park is the perfect place to spend a sunny afternoon. There are plenty of beautiful spots for picnics, and you can go hiking on a number of trails. The trails will take you to interesting spots throughout the park, such as the Gettysburg National Cemetery, where the casualties of the battle are buried.

Independence National Historical Park
Open year-round, 9 a.m. to 5 p.m. daily. Located at 3rd Street in Philadelphia. Call (215) 627-1776. There is an admission fee of $2 for each adult and $1 for each child. This park is comprised of several sites of historical signifi-

cance in Philadelphia, the hub of modern thinking in colonial America. All of the sites are indicative of the spirit that caused America to grow and become independent, such as Congress Hall and Independence Hall. This is a wonderful tour you will never forget, and it will forever change your conception of what a park has to be.

Valley Forge National Historical Park
Open year-round, 8:30 a.m. to 5 p.m. daily. Located on Valley Forge Road in Valley Forge. Call (215) 783-1077. There is an admission charge of $1 for each adult. This park is situated on the exact spot where the Revolutionary Army survived the grueling winter of 1777-8. Many of the soldiers' living quarters are still standing, as is the building that George Washington used for his headquarters. There are many lovely spots for picnics, and you can even hike over a variety of trails, well suited to all levels of experience, which will take you to historic locations. You can also fish and boat in the nearby waters. Actors in period clothing even reenact scenes from when the soldiers struggled to overcome the cold.

Amusement Parks

Dorney Park

Open from April to Labor Day, 10 a.m. to 10 p.m. daily. Located at 3830 Dorney Park Road in Allentown. Call (215) 398-7955. There is an admission charge of $20. In operation for 130 years, this wet and dry park has evolved and perfected itself until the point where it's hard to find a single fault with it! It features almost 45 rides, one-third of which are designed especially for younger children. Some of the more popular rides include a Ferris wheel, bumper cars, a train ride, and several spectacular roller coasters. You can also challenge your friends and family to a round of mini-golf, test your aim at the shooting gallery, and speed along the park in a go-kart or speedboat!

Hersheypark

Open from May to September, 10 a.m. to 10 p.m. daily. Located at 100 West Hersheypark Drive in Hershey. Call (717) 534-3824. There is an admission charge of $20. If you're wondering why this park is called Hersheypark, it's because it was founded by Milton Hershey, the chocolate magnate. A splendid and fairly large park, it has the added bonus of its own zoo, where you can encounter cuddly or ferocious animals! It features over 50 rides, about one-fourth of which are designed especially for younger children. Some of the more popular rides include a Ferris wheel, several terrific roller coasters, a carousel, and a log ride. You can also challenge your friends and family to a round of mini-golf, go on a tour of a real chocolate factory (yum), and go for a leisurely ride in a paddleboat. You musn't forget to visit the wonderful zoo!

Kennywood
Open from May to Labor Day, noon to 11 p.m. daily. Located on Route 837 in West Mifflin. Call (412) 461-0500. You can either buy an unlimited ride pass for $15, or you can pay for each ride separately, but parking is free. About to celebrate its one-hundredth anniversary in the coming years, this wonderful park is already considered a National Landmark. Its early-1900s architecture is the home to over 50 rides, about one-third of which are designed especially for young children. Some of the more popular rides include several incredible roller coasters (one of which is the world's fastest!), a carousel, a haunted house, and a log ride. You can also take a paddleboat out for a spin in the pond, and challenge your family and friends to a round of mini-golf.

RHODE ISLAND

Attractions

Arcade
Open year-round, every day. Located at 65 Weybosset Street in Providence. Call (401) 272-2340. Free. If you want to combine sightseeing and shopping, then this is definitely the place for you! The oldest shopping mall in the country (construction began 150 years ago!), it features some of the best shops in the state. The architecture is fabulous.

Colonial Newport
Open year-round, every day (weekends only during April and October). Located in Newport, starting on Washington Street. Call (401) 847-1000. There is a charge for some of the attractions. Virtually an outdoor museum, this small section of the town features many buildings of historical significance. Most have been restored entirely, and include antique furniture and clothing so that you can see what it was really like to live centuries ago!

Founders Brook
Always open. Located off Boyd's Lane in Portsmouth. Free. This is one of the most historically significant sites in the country. It is where Anne Hutchinson created the town of

Portsmouth in 1638 (the first American woman with so much authority). The government she created to run her town was the first true democracy of all time.

Museum of Yachting
Open year-round, 9 a.m. to 5 p.m. Tuesday to Sunday. Located on Ocean Drive in Newport. Call (401) 847-1018. The home of the America's Cup, Rhode Island is no stranger to yachting. And you can experience the history of this exciting sport by visiting this museum, housed in a beautiful structure. Not only will you see wonderful artwork, but you can even view some of the most famous ships to ever sail the high seas.

Newport Art Museum and Art Association
Open year-round, 10 a.m. to 5 p.m. Tuesday to Saturday, 1 p.m. to 5 p.m. Sunday. Located at 76 Bellevue Avenue in Newport. Call (401) 847-0179. There is an admission charge of $2.50. One of the most beautiful buildings on the East Coast, Stanford White's Newport Casino contains a beautiful collection of art. If you're an art lover, then this is a must-see!

Old State House
Open year-round, every day. Located at 150 Benefit Street in Portsmouth. Free. A site of true

historical significance for mankind, this is where colonists first declared themselves independent from Britain, prior to drafting the actual Declaration of Independence.

Providence Athenaeum
Open year-round, Tuesday to Sunday. Located at 251 Benefit Street in Providence. Call (401) 421-6970. Free. Featuring many rare and fine books (not to mention a substantial art collection) this is one of the first libraries in the world. If you're a book lover, and you must be since you're reading this, then you shouldn't miss a visit here.

State House
Open year-round, 9 a.m. to 5 p.m. weekdays. Located on Smith Street in Providence. Call (401) 277-2357. If you want to see a real piece of history, then you should definitely come here! Under one of the biggest dome roofs in the world sits the charter that King Charles of England signed enabling Rhode Island to become a colony in the New World!

Historic Sites and Monuments

Roger Williams National Memorial
Open year-round, 8 a.m. to 4:30 p.m. daily.

Located on Smith Street in Providence. Call (401) 528-5385. Free. The colony of Rhode Island was founded by Roger Williams, an ardent proponent of the freedom of religion. This memorial commemorates his life and achievements. There are many displays about the founding of the colony.

Touro Synagogue National Historic Site
Open year-round, 1 p.m. to 3 p.m. Sunday (open daily at various times during the year, so call first). Located on Touro Street in Newport. Call (401) 847-4794. Free. The first synagogue built in the country, this site is a testament to the religious freedom found in the United States. Rhode Island is particularly proud of this site, as the original colony was founded by people fleeing religious persecution. You can take a guided tour of this building, featuring magnificent architecture and beautiful furnishings.

Amusement Parks

Rocky Point Park
Open from April to September, noon to 10:30 p.m. daily. Located on Rocky Point Avenue in Warwick. Call (401) 737-8000. You can either

buy an unlimited ride pass for $10, or you can pay for each ride separately, but parking is free. Situated on well over 100 acres, and well over 100 years old, this is a splendid amusement park with a traditional atmosphere! It features almost 35 rides, about one-third of which are designed especially for younger children. Some of the more popular rides include a log ride, a terrific roller coaster, and a chilling haunted house. You can sit back and watch one of the several fun shows presented each day, such as foot-stompin' musicals. You can eat at any of over 15 restaurants, including the *huge* (who thought anything in Rhode Island could be huge?) Shore Dinner Hall, which specializes in succulent seafood.

TRAVEL GUIDE TO THE UNITED STATES

SOUTH CAROLINA

Attractions

Burt-Starke Mansion
Open year-round, by appointment only. Located at 1865 North Main Street in Abbeville. Call (803) 459-4297. Free. One of the most historically significant houses in the country, this is where Jefferson Davis, president of the Confederacy, last met with his cabinet members before the end of the Civil War. The house itself is exquisite, and it is furnished with many antiques.

Charleston Museum
Open year-round, 9 a.m. to 5 p.m. daily. Located at 360 Meeting Street in Charleston. Call (803) 722-2996. There is an admission charge of $8 for adults and $5 for kids. The oldest urban museum in America, this popular tourist site features more than just paintings. You can sample all facets of culture, from old toys and games to trends in clothing.

Charleston Naval Base
Open year-round, 1 p.m. to 4 p.m. Saturday and Sunday. Located on Viaduct Road in Charleston. Call (803) 743-3940. Free. If you're a fan of military ships, then this tour is for you! You'll get to see the functionings of a real navy base and even walk through a huge battleship.

Old City Market
Located near Meeting Street in Charleston. If you want to spend a lovely afternoon shopping, then don't miss the Old City Market. Featuring some of the finest shops and restaurants in the city, you can even buy fruits and veggies from vendors (what a relief from hotel food!). Don't forget to buy some regional arts and crafts.

The South Carolina State Museum
Open year-round, 9 a.m. to 5 p.m. daily. Located at 301 Gervais Street in Columbia. Call (803) 737-4921. There is an admission charge of $5. If you want to learn more about the fascinating state of South Carolina, then this museum will tell you all you need to know. Its displays cover all facets of the state's evolution, from art to archaeology.

Riverbanks Zoological Park
Open year-round, every day. Located at Greystone Boulevard in Columbia. Call (803) 779-8717. One of the finest zoos in the area, this attraction will not disappoint you! Featuring thousands of animals, many of which come from endangered species, you can see birds, mammals, reptiles, and a host of other creatures. There is even a splendid aquarium. A perfect place to spend the day with your family.

Historic Sites and Monuments

Charles Pinckney National Historical Site
Open year-round, every day. Located off of Longpoint Road in Mount Pleasant. Free. This site commemorates the achievements of Charles Pinckney by preserving the house in which he lived. Pinckney was not only a Revolutionary War hero and one of the authors of the Constitution, he was also a governor, congressman, and presidential aid.

Congaree Swamp National Monument
Always open. Located off Highway 48 a few miles south of Columbia. Call (803) 776-4396. Free. If you're a nature lover, then this is the place for you. Featuring a wide variety of flora and fauna, this site preserves many precious and endangered species. Great for weekend camping trips or afternoon picnics.

Fort Sumter National Monument
Open year-round, 9 a.m. to 5 p.m. daily. Located on Sullivan's Island in Charleston Harbor (you have to take a boat). Call (803) 883-3123. There is a charge of $8 for each adult and $4 for each kid to take the boat. This site is historically significant due to its roles in two of the most important wars in American history. It was here that that the first shots of the Civil War were

fired, and Fort Moultrie, which adjoins Fort Sumter, was the site of a major British defeat in the Revolutionary War.

Ninety Six National Historic Site
Open year-round, 8 a.m. to 5 p.m. daily. Located off Route 248 just south of Ninety Six. Call (803) 543-4068. Free. One of the most important trading sites in the Colonial Period, this region was bitterly fought over during the Revolution. Remnants of the battles, such as foxholes, still exist.

National Parks and Recreation Areas

Kings Mountain National Military Park
Open year-round, 9 a.m. to 5 p.m. daily (extended hours during the summer). Located off of Interstate 85 in Kings Mountain. Call (803) 936-7921. Free. Visit the site of one of the most important battles of the Revolutionary War. When the colonial militia overcame British forces, Thomas Jefferson knew that they had won their independence! The park is a great place to spend the afternoon, and several trails will lead you to the most important sites of the battlefield. You can also watch a short film about the park, and even go horseback riding.

Amusement Parks

**Myrtle Beach Pavilion
and Amusement Park**
Open from March to September, 1 p.m. to midnight daily. Located at the intersection of 9th and Ocean Avenues in Myrtle Beach. Call (803) 448-6456. You can either pay for each ride individually, or you can buy an unlimited ride pass for $15. There is also a charge for parking. This small park surely isn't small on fun! Situated in the greater downtown portion of Myrtle Beach, this seashore park can make a wonderful break from sightseeing. It features over 30 rides, such as roller coasters and carousels. There's also a video game arcade (it's huge!) and you can challenge your friends and family to a round of mini-golf. You might even happen to visit the park on a day when a famous singer is performing! You can eat at any of over 20 locations, so you won't leave the park feeling hungry.

TRAVEL GUIDE TO THE UNITED STATES

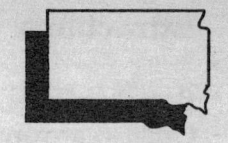

SOUTH DAKOTA

Attractions

Bramble Park Zoo
Open year-round, 8 a.m. to 11 p.m. daily. Located on 10th Avenue West in Watertown. Free. This charming little zoo has all the animals you'd expect, as well as a few you might never have seen before: buffalo!

Dakota Territorial Museum
Open from Memorial Day to Labor Day, 1 p.m. to 5 p.m. daily. Only open by appointment at other times in the year. Free, but donations are accepted. This museum brings the first pioneers of Wisconsin to life. Exhibits include the tools they used to survive their arduous lifestyles.

Earth Resources Observation System Data Center
Open year-round, 8 a.m. to 4:15 p.m. weekdays. Located on County Road 121, a short distance outside of Sioux Falls. Call (605) 594-6511. Tour one of the country's most important satellite information retrieval centers. There are plenty of really exciting things to see and do.

Fort Randall Dam
Open year-round, 8 a.m. to 4:30 p.m. daily. Located on Route 281 just west of Pickstown. Call (605) 487-7844. Free. Tour a working dam

and discover the complexities of its functions. Learn more about hydro-electric power through fun and informative demonstrations and interactive exhibits.

Historic District of Yankton
Open year-round, every day. Located on Mulberry and Cedar Streets in Yankton. Free. Watch history come to life before your very eyes in the town that was South Dakota's territorial capitol. There are many buildings you can tour and examine that are over one hundred years old.

McCrory Gardens
Open year-round, dawn to dusk daily. Located at South Dakota State University, on 6th Street. Call (605) 688-5136. Free. If you are interested in flowers, then this is the place for you. Scientists at this university study plant life and develop new strains of seeds. The best time to visit is during the summer.

Mount Moriah Cemetery
Open year-round, dawn to dusk daily. Located just outside of Deadwood. Free from November through May. Visit the final resting places of some of the most famous heroes and outlaws of the Old West. Just two of the notorious permanent residents of this graveyard are Wild Bill Hickock and Calamity Jane.

Pettigrew Home
Open year-round, 9 a.m. to 5 p.m. Monday to Saturday, 2 p.m. to 5 p.m. Sunday. Located at 131 North Duluth in Sioux Falls. Call (605) 339-7097. Free. This beautiful 110 year old Victorian-style house belonged to the first senator of South Dakota. It also has a museum with displays about regional history dating back to the Native Americans.

Sitting Bull's Grave
Open year-round, every day. Located west of Mobridge off of Route 12. Free. Visit the grave of one of the most well-known Native Americans. There is an impressive statue commemorating the warrior chief.

State Capitol Building
Open year-round, 8 a.m. to 5 p.m. weekdays. Located on Capitol Avenue. Call (605) 773-3011. This building, over 80 years old, showcases the history of the state. It features gorgeous architecture, accented by stained glass.

Wounded Knee Battlefield
Open year-round, every day. Located on the Pine Ridge Reservation, near Pine Ridge. Free. Visit the field where the final conflict of the Indian Wars took place. This is where General George Custer last saw the light of day.

Historic Sites and Monuments

Battleship U.S.S. South Dakota Memorial
Open from Memorial Day to Labor Day, 9 a.m. to 5 p.m. daily. Located off of Interstate 29, just east of Sioux Falls. Call (605) 339-7060. This memorial commemorates the famous battleship that served during World War II.

Fort Meade
Open year-round, every day. Located almost 40 miles east of Sturgis, off of Route 18. Free. This fort was important from the late 1800s through World War II. It played a crucial role in the Wounded Knee unrest.

Jewel Cave National Monument
Open year-round, every day. Located about 10 miles west of Custer on Route 16. Call (605) 673-2288. There is a charge of $2 to $4 for each person going on a tour. Many beautiful caves have been formed by the natural erosion of limestone. The name comes from the fact that some of the caves sparkle like jewels.

Mount Rushmore National Memorial
Open year-round, 8 a.m. to 5 p.m. daily (8 a.m. to 10 p.m. daily from May to September). Located on Route 244, several miles south of

Keystone. Call (605) 574-2523. Free. This world-famous memorial features the humongous faces of Presidents Roosevelt, Lincoln, Jefferson, and Washington carved into the side of a mountain. Not to be missed!

National Parks and Recreation Areas

Badlands National Park

Open year-round, every day, but sudden extremes in weather can cause closure unexpectedly. Located just outside of Interior on Route SH240. Call (605) 433-5361. There is an admission charge of $1 for each individual or $3 for each car, and an additional charge of $7 for camping. This beautiful park features vast prairies where you can observe herds of buffalo. It also features fossils that date back almost 40 million years. The park is perfect for hiking, camping, and climbing, and there are many tours of the fossil beds. There are miles of hiking trails, well suited to all levels of experience, and there are many campsites. You can also hike in the backcountry. There is also a lodge in the park with a restaurant in it.

TRAVEL GUIDE TO THE UNITED STATES

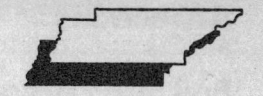

TENNESSEE

Attractions

Beal Street Historic District
Open year-round, every day. Located in downtown Memphis. If you want to experience some Tennessee nightlife, then this is definitely the district to visit. You'll find many of Memphis' finest stores and restaurants here, not to mention several important museums.

Civil Rights Museum
Open year-round, 9 a.m. to 5 p.m. Wednesday to Monday. Located at 450 Mulberry Street in Memphis. Call (901) 521-9699. Monday afternoons are free. Truly one of the most important sites in the country, this museum celebrates the civil rights movement and the accomplishments of Dr. Martin Luther King, Jr. The museum is located in the building where Dr. King was shot and killed.

Country Music Hall of Fame
Open year-round, 9 a.m. to 5 p.m. daily. Located at 4 Music Square East in Nashville. Call (615) 256-1639. There is an admission charge of $10. If you love country music, then it's a crime for you to miss this landmark! You can learn everything there is to know about this rip-roarin' type of music, and you can even visit a studio where Country greats like Dolly Parton have recorded!

Graceland

Open year-round, Wednesday to Monday. Located at 3717 Elvis Presley Boulevard in Memphis. Call (901) 332-3322. There is an admission charge of $10. One of the most popular tourist sites in the world, you musn't leave Tennessee without first visiting the home of the King of Rock and Roll! There are always thousands of Elvis fans lining up to go here, however, so don't forget to make a reservation.

Jack Daniel Distillery

Open year-round, 8 a.m. to 4 p.m. daily. Located on Route 55, a few miles north of Lynchberg. Call (615) 759-4221, extension 312. Free. The oldest and most famous distillery in the country, Jack Daniels has become an American tradition. You can tour the facility and see just how Mr. Daniel's whiskey is made.

Memphis Zoological Gardens and Aquarium

Open year-round, 9 a.m. to 5 p.m. daily. Located at 2000 Galloway Avenue in Memphis. Call (901) 726-4775. This huge zoo is one of the best places to visit while you're in Tennessee. Your whole family will enjoy watching thousands of animals in their native habitats, including an enormous section devoted solely to wild cats!

State Capitol

Open year-round, 9 a.m. to 5 p.m. daily. Located on Charlotte Avenue in Nashville. Call (615) 741-0830. Free. This beautiful building, penned by world renowned architect William Strickland, is a sight to behold! Its fantastic lines are reminiscent of classical Greek buildings. You can even visit the tomb of President James Polk, who was a native of Tennessee.

Historic Sites and Monuments

Andrew Johnson National Historic Site

Open year-round, 9 a.m. to 5 p.m. daily. Located on Depot Street in Greeneville. Call (615) 638-3551. There is an admission charge for adults. This site commemorates the achievements of President Andrew Johnson by preserving his home, his place of business, and his final resting place.

Fort Donelson National Battlefield

Open year-round, 8 a.m. to 4:30 p.m. daily. Located just west of the town square in Dover. Call (615) 232-5348. Free. Visit the site of Ulysses S. Grant's first significant victory in the Civil War. Under his leadership, Union soldiers crushed Confederate forces in 1862.

Stones River
National Battlefield and Cemetery

Open year-round, 8 a.m. to 5 p.m. daily. Located in Murfreesboro. Call (615) 893-9501. Free. Visit the site of one of the most important battles in the Civil War! In 1862, Union soldiers began to overcome the Confederacy by cutting their forces off from each other. They continued to divide the Southern troops until the Union's victory was inevitable. There is also a cemetery here.

National Parks and Recreation Areas

Big South Fork
National River and Recreation Area

Always open. Located off of Route 297 in Oneida. Call (615) 569-9778. Free. This recently created National Park encompasses the Cumberland River's entire Big South Fork. As such, the rafting, canoeing, swimming, and fishing are all excellent. There are almost 150 miles of hiking trails, well suited to all levels of experience. You can also camp at one of several different campsites, or you can rough it out in the back country if you are a more experienced camper. There are many lovely spots that are perfect for picnicking.

Great Smoky Mountains National Park

Always open. Located just north of Gatlinburg on Route 441. Call (615) 436-1200. There is a charge of $8-$11 for camping, collected nightly. One of the largest mountain ranges in the country, Great Smoky is a wonder to behold! It is a haven for many animals and plants that you might not see anywhere else. There are almost one thousand miles of trails, perfect for both horseback riding and hiking. The fishing is great in the many streams within the park, and nature lovers often bring their cameras to capture the wildlife on film. You can camp at one of several campsites, or you can even go out into the backcountry. There are also a few hotels and lodges available, but remember to make reservations well in advance.

Shiloh National Military Park

Open year-round, 8 a.m. to 5 p.m. daily. Located on Route 64, just south of Adamsville. (901) 689-5275. There is a $1 admission charge for each adult. Visit the site of one of the most important conflicts in the Civil War, in which Ulysses S. Grant defeated Confederate troops. This park is an entertaining and educational place to visit. You can walk along many guided trails, stopping at areas of significance on the battlefield. The many grassy fields also make a lovely picnic area.

Amusement Parks

Dollywood
Open from April to October and Thanksgiving to Christmas, 8:30 a.m. to 7 p.m. daily. Located at 700 Dollywood Lane in Pigeon Forge. Call (615) 428-9488. There is an admission charge of around $20, and an additional charge for parking. If you're into country music, then this large park is right up you're alley! Dolly Parton has created a good ol' place to visit, showcasing the traditions of the area in which she was raised. She even appears in the park quite frequently. There are over 15 rides, about one-third of which are designed especially for younger children. Some of the more popular rides include an incredible roller coaster, a fun old train ride, and a raging water ride. You'll always find a famous country singer strutting his or her stuff up on the stage, and you can even tour a museum commemorating Dolly's achievements. And don't forget to take a look at the beautiful birds in the aviary. To top it all off, you can pan for gold and practice your marksmanship. There are about 15 places where you can sit down to some delicious country-style cooking, including a fabulous barbecued pork dinner. Y'all come back now, y'hear?!

Opryland

Open from March to October, 9 a.m. to 9 p.m. daily. Located at 2802 Opry land Drive in Nashville. Call (615) 889-6600. There is an admission charge of $25, and an additional charge for parking. Tennessee is truly the home of country music, and this fun filled theme park commemorating this popular music will make you glad you're a fan. Its beautiful grounds feature almost 25 rides, many of which are designed specifically for younger children. Some of the more enjoyable rides include fun old trains, a fantastic indoor roller coaster (it'll knock your socks off!), and a raging water ride. Don't forget to stop by the zoo and pet some cute and cuddly critters; a museum honoring some of country's finest celebrities rounds out the park's regular attractions. There are dozens of different country music shows that rotate daily, but rest assured that every single one of them is a blast. Really famous singers are always dropping by, so you might get to see one of your favorite performers in concert. There are about a dozen different places in which you can eat, so prepare yourself for some good grub.

TRAVEL GUIDE TO THE UNITED STATES

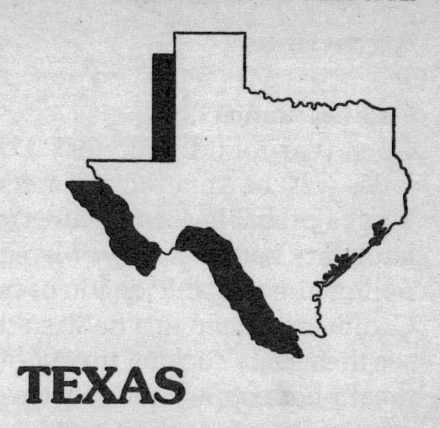

TEXAS

Attractions

Cadillac Ranch
Open year-round, every day. Located a few miles west of Amarillo on Interstate 40. Free. You've probably seen pictures of this odd landmark before. Stanley Marsh III, eccentric millionaire and afficionado of pop art, had 10 Cadillacs planted in a field, so that you can just see their rears sticking up out of the ground. A great photo opportunity that is sure to make conversation for years to come.

Fair Park
Open year-round, every day. Located at 1300 Robert B. Cullum Boulevard in Dallas. Call (214) 670-8400. If you want to pack a whole lot of fun into one day, then this is definitely the place to visit! This huge park contains the Museum of African American Life and Culture, the Dallas Civic Garden Center, the Dallas Aquarium, the Science Place, the Railroad Museum, and much more! Times and admission prices vary, so don't forget to call first.

Houston Zoo
Open year-round, every day. Located at 1513 North MacGregor in Houston. Call (713) 639-4629. As well as having the opportunity to see plenty of ferocious and exotic animals, you can

also visit an aquarium in this zoo. There's even a petting zoo for the little ones, and a few small amusement park-style rides.

Lyndon Baines Johnson Library
Open year-round, 9 a.m. to 5 p.m. Located at 2313 Red River Street in Austin. Call (512) 397-5279. Free. Lyndon Johnson was president during one of the most turbulent eras of American history. As such, this museum commemorating his achievements is a fascinating place to visit. You can see many of his personal belongings, as well as learn more about his time in office.

Museum of Natural History
Open year-round, 9 a.m. to 5 p.m. daily. Located at 1 Hermann Circle Drive in Houston. Call (713) 639-4629. Considered to be one of the finest museums of science in the country, this attraction is not to be missed! Don't forget to catch a fascinating show in the gigantic-screen movie theatre, and you'll love their famous planetarium.

San Antonio Museum of the Arts
Open year-round, every day. Located at 200 West Jones Avenue in San Antonio. Call (512) 226-5544. There is an admission charge of $5. If you're an art lover, then you won't want to miss

this fabulous museum. It features the works of many Southwestern artists, some dating back to before the arrival of Columbus!

Tower of the Americas
Open year-round, every day. Located in Hemisfair Park in San Antonio. Call (512) 226-7651. Free. One of the most popular landmarks in San Antonio, this impressive tower has an incredible view of the city!

Historic Sites and Monuments

Alibates Flint Quarries
National Monument
Open from Memorial Day to Labor Day, every day. Located on Alibates Road just south of Fritch. Call (806) 857-3151. Free. For over 10 millennia before the arrival of Europeans, Native Americans mined this site for dolomite stone to make weapons and tools. This was possibly the most important place to Native Americans of the region.

Chamizal National Memorial
Open year-round, 8 a.m. to 5 p.m. daily. Located on San Marcial Street in El Paso. Call (915) 532-7273. Free. This site honors the peaceful relations enjoyed by Mexico and the United

States since 1963. Prior to that point, there had still been much animosity over Texas and other Southwestern regions. If you want to watch a performance celebrating the rich cultures of Mexico and the American Southwest, then there is no better place to go than here (there is a charge for such presentations)!

Fort Davis National Historic Site
Open year-round, 8 a.m. to 5 p.m. daily. Located in Fort Davis. Call (915) 426-3225. There is an admission charge of $1 for each individual. This fort was one of the major American posts in Texas during the 1800s. It features dramatic Southwestern architecture and restored interiors. A fascinating glimpse into the lives of soldiers of the 19th century.

National Parks and Recreation Areas

Amistad National Recreation Area
Open year-round, 8 a.m. to 5 p.m. daily. Located on Highway 90, a few miles west of Del Rio. Call (512) 775-7491. Free. This recently created Recreation Area is a large reservoir resulting from the Amistad Dam (which collects water from the Pecos, Devil's, and Rio Grande Rivers). As a result, the boating, sailing, fishing,

waterskiing, and swimming are unbelievable! There are no hiking trails, but the backcountry is splendid if you are a more experienced hiker. In addition, there are several campsites, or you can camp in the backcountry if you prefer. You should be aware that part of this park extends into Mexican territory and, as a result, you might have to buy some Mexican permits.

Big Bend National Park
Always open. Located 25 miles east of Study Butte, off Highway 385. Call (915) 477-2251. There is a charge for admission, and an additional charge for camping. This National Park is stunningly beautiful due to the juxtaposition of mountain and desert terrains. There are a tremendous amount of hiking trails, well suited to all levels of experience, and some of them are also great for horseback riding. You can go fishing or boating in the river, and you can camp at any of several campsites. If you are a more experienced camper, then you might even want to go into the backcountry. There is also a lodge where you can spend the night.

Guadalupe Mountains National Park
Open year-round, 8:30 a.m. to 4:30 p.m. daily. Located about 100 miles east of El Paso on Highway 62-180. Call (915) 828-3251. There is a camping charge of $5, collected nightly. This

park is world renowned for the splendor of the mountains that seem to rise straight out of the desert sands. The park is best known for its hiking, and there are almost one hundred miles of trails, well suited to all levels of experience, for you to tackle. Some of the trails are also great for horseback riding. You can camp at a number of different campsites, or you can venture out into the backcountry (but there is a special release that you must sign). Beware of sudden changes in weather conditions.

Lake Meredith National Recreation Area
Always open. Located in Fritch, on Highway 136. Call (806) 857-3151. Free. If you enjoy water sports, then this artificial lake is like heaven on earth! Swimming, scuba diving, boating sailing, water skiing, and fishing are all as good as possible in this recreation area. There are no hiking trails, but you can get maps to hike through the backcountry. You can spend the night in one of the designated campsites, or you can even bring your tent with you into the backcountry. Beware of sudden changes in weather conditions.

San Antonio Missions
National Historical Park
Open year-round, 9 a.m. to 6 p.m. daily. Located at 2202 Roosevelt Avenue in San Antonio.

Call (512) 229-5701. Free. If you've always wanted to see the world famous Alamo where Davy Crockett finally met his maker, then don't miss this park. It commemorates the many 18th century Spanish missions in the area, including the Alamo. You can spend a truly fascinating afternoon examining and touring these buildings.

Amusement Parks

Sandy Lake Amusement Park
Open from Easter to September, 10 a.m. to 6 p.m. daily. Located at 1800 Sandy Lake Road in Dallas. Call (214) 242-7449. There is a reasonable charge for admission, and an additional charge for each ride, but parking is free. This large amusement park is a great place to take your family for a fun filled afternoon. It features almost 30 rides, including bumper cars, a fun house, and a roller coaster designed especially for younger children. You can also ride a pony and challenge your family and friends to a round of mini-golf. If you feel like going for a swim, then this place has one of the biggest swimming pools you'll ever see in your whole life. There are about 5 snack bars for you to eat at, and health conscious people will be happy to learn that none of the food is fried.

Sea World of Texas

Open from March to November, 10 a.m. to 11 p.m. daily. Located at 10500 Sea World Drive in San Antonio. Call (512) 523-3600. There is an admission charge of $25, but parking is free. Visiting any Sea World park is probably the most fun you'll ever have learning about our friends who inhabit the oceans. The park only features two rides on its huge grounds (both are excellent water rides that are not to be missed), but there are plenty of shows to entertain and inform you. It would be a crime for you to leave without paying a visit to Shamu the killer whale, and the other shows are great too. Many times children from the audience are even invited to participate! You can eat at any of over 15 different restaurants.

Six Flags Astro World

Open from March to October, 11 a.m. to 11 p.m. daily (midnight on weekends). Located at 9001 Kirby Drive in Houston. Call (713) 799-1234. There is an admission charge of $25, and an additional charge for parking. This large theme park encapsulates the history of America in all its glory. Its beautiful grounds, which feature some of the most gorgeous landscaping and flower gardens you will ever set your eyes on, is the home to over 30 rides. Some of the more popular rides include a twisting roller coaster, a wooden roller coaster, a carousel, and a cable car. You should take in as many of the 11 shows as you can, because they're all great; they feature everything from trained dolphins to gunfights. If you're lucky, you might even happen to be in the park on a day when a famous singer is giving a concert! There are almost 40 different places to eat, offering everything from quick snacks to full meals.

Six Flags Over Texas
Open from April to October, 10 a.m to about 8 p.m. daily. Located at 2201 Road to Six Flags in Arlington. Call (817) 640-8900. There is an admission charge of $20, and an additional charge for parking. The oldest of the Six Flags operations, this huge amusement park is still one of the best in the country! It features almost 35 rides in its beautiful grounds, 6 of which are designed specifically for younger children. Some of the more popular rides include several world famous roller coasters, a carousel, a fun little train ride (one of the first rides in the park), and a raging water ride. There are almost 10 shows for you to watch, and I suggest you catch as many of them as possible. The dolphin show is really great, as are the costumed Looney Tunes performers. You can eat at any of almost 40 places, offering everything from snacks and fast food to healthy meals.

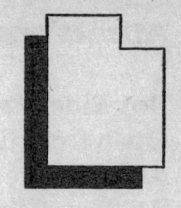

UTAH

Attractions

Box Elder Tabernacle
Open from June to August, 8 a.m. to 8 p.m. daily. Located at 251 South Main Street in Brigham City. Tours are free. This magnificent temple is over one hundred years old. Beautiful architecture!

Daughters of Utah Pioneer's Museum
Open June to August, 1 p.m. to 5 p.m. weekdays; you must make an appointment during other months. Located at 52 West 200 North Street in Logan. Call (801) 752-2161. Free. This museum commemorates the pioneers and founders of Utah and includes many items of historical significance.

Hamblin Home
Open year-round, weekdays. Located west of Santa Clara in Dixie State Park. This museum was the home of Jacob Hamblin, one of the most influential Mormon missionaries.

Kennecott Mine
Open year-round, every day. Located near Bingham Canyon. Call (801) 263-6123. A viewing deck above the opening to the world's biggest open-pit copper mine provides you with an interesting sight.

Temple Square
Open year-round, 8 a.m. to 8:30 p.m. daily. Located at Main Street and South Temple in Salt Lake City. Free. Guided tours are available of this Mormon (Latter-Day Saints) center. They run throughout the day, and you can visit several huge temples and sites within the square.

Topaz War Relocation Center
Open year-round. Located about fifteen miles north of Delta. This is the infamous site where almost ten thousand Japanese-Americans were jailed in 1942 and 1943 by Executive Order.

Historic Sites and Monuments

Cedar Breaks National Monument
Open June to October, 8 a.m. to 6 p.m. daily; only open during rest of the year if weather permits. Located about 15 miles from Parowan, off of Route 143. Call (801) 586-9451. $3 charge for each vehicle, and additional charges for camping. Yet another astonishing natural formation in Utah, this monument is an amphitheater that has formed within the Pink Cliffs. Wonderful camping and hiking trails are available.

Golden Spike National Historic Site
Open year-round, 8 a.m. to 4:30 p.m. daily (8 a.m. to 6 p.m. during the summer months). Located off Route 13/83, 30 miles west of Brigham City. Call (801) 471-2209. $1 entry fee for each adult, or $3 for each car. This is the exact site where the Union Pacific and Central Pacific Railroads joined together and drove the Golden Spike in 1869, forming the first transcontinental railway. Features tours and locomotives (from May to early October).

Rainbow Bridge National Monument
Always open. Located near Lake Powell (most people use boats to reach the monument). Call (602) 645-2471 for precise directions. Free. This natural bridge crosses 290 feet above Bridge Canyon. It is made of pink stone, and it is widely considered one of the most beautiful natural formations in existence.

National Parks and Recreation Areas

Arches National Park
Always open, and the weather is usually temperate throughout the year. Located on Route 191, just outside of Moab. Call (801) 259-8161. There is an admission charge of $3 for each

vehicle or $1 for each individual, and an additional charge of up to $7 for camping. This national park contains many colorful and unique topographical features, such as arches, formed through natural erosion. There are plenty of hiking trails, and you can also hike through the backcountry. There are also many tours of the arches. Campsites are available, but there are no cabins or lodges.

Bryce Canyon National Park
Open year-long, every day, but inclement weather forces closure of some areas during the winter. Located on Route 63 in Bryce Canyon. Call (801) 834-5322. There is an admission charge of $5 for each vehicle or $2 for each person, and an additional charge of $6 for camping. The beautiful features of this national park form incredible amphitheatre-shaped pockets. Park rangers give frequent tours and presentations of the natural history of the area. There are many hiking trails, but some are quite difficult due to their slope. There are plenty of campsites for you to spend the night, and there is a lodge open from May to September.

Zion National Park
Always open, but inclement weather can force closure during any season. Located on Route 9 in Springdale. Call (801) 772-3256. There is an

admission charge of $5 for each vehicle or $2 for each individual, and an additional charge of $6 for camping. This beautiful national park contains desert terrain in all its glory. The hiking is incredible, either on clearly marked trails or through the backcountry. There are plenty of natural formations for mountain climbing, and park rangers put on presentations daily. You can camp at a campsite, or you can make reservations at Zion Lodge.

Amusement Parks

Lagoon Park
Open from April to October, 11 a.m. to midnight daily. Located at I-15 and Lagoon Drive in Farmington. Call (801) 451-0101. Admission is $20, and there is a fee for parking. This immense amusement park rivals the best from across the country. The park features over 40 rides, including several roller coasters, a train, and the mysterious Dracula's Castle. There is also a fairly large water area which features many aquatic rides. Mother Gooseland is an area for the little ones, with rides designed just for them. Don't miss Pioneer Village, a recreation of the homesteads of the earliest settlers of the state. On top of all this there are petting zoos, gunfights, musicals, and clowns.

TRAVEL GUIDE TO THE UNITED STATES

VERMONT

Attractions

Bennington Museum
Open year-round, every day. Located on West Main Street in Bennington. Call (802) 447-1571. If you want to learn more about early America, then this is the place to visit. Featuring all sorts of folk art and everyday items of the past, a trip here makes a fascinating and fun-filled afternoon.

Robert Hull Fleming Museum
Open year-round, 9 a.m. to 5 p.m. daily. Located on Colchester Avenue in Burlington. Call (802) 656-0750. This fantastic museum lets you explore the history of culture in the state of Vermont dating all the way back to prehistoric Native American times! Examples of exhibits include old arrowheads and pottery.

Museum of American Flyfishing
Open year-round, 9 a.m. to 5 p.m. daily. Located on Route 7 just south of Manchester. Call (802) 362-3300. Donations requested. If you're a fisherman, then you don't want to miss this great place! You can learn more about the history of your favorite sport, including the evolution of the equipment.

Saint Johnsbury Athenaeum
Open year-round, 9 a.m. to 5 p.m. daily. Located at 30 Main Street in Saint Johnsbury. Call (802) 748-8291. Free. One of the most beautiful structures on the East Coast, you won't be disappointed by a trip here! As well as marvelling at the architecture, you can also view some photos by Albert Bierstadt, considered to be some of the finest in the world.

State Capitol Building
Open year-round, 8 a.m. to 4 p.m. daily. Located on Capitol Street in Montpelier. Call (802) 828-1110. Free. One of the most beautiful buildings in the state, it's filled with valuable artwork and antiques. The highly ornate architecture is inspired by classical Greek design.

Vermont Institute of Natural Science's Raptor Center
Open year-round, 9 a.m. to 5 p.m. daily. Located on Church Hill Road in Woodstock. Call (802) 457-2779. There is a $5 charge for admission. If you love finding out more about nature and the world around you, then a trip here is definitely in order. While touring a variety of wooded trails, you can encounter and study many different birds indigenous to the region. This is a great way to get away from the hustle and bustle of the city.

TRAVEL GUIDE TO THE UNITED STATES

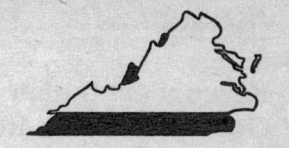

VIRGINIA

Attractions

Kecoughtan Indian Village
Open year-round, 10 a.m. to 3 p.m. Monday to Saturday, noon to 4 p.m. Sunday. Located at 418 West Mercury Boulevard in Hampton. Call (804) 727-6248. Free. This recreated Native American village is a fascinating place to visit. Accurate to the smallest detail, you will gain tremendous insight into the beautiful culture and way of life of these people.

Mount Vernon
Open year-round, 9 a.m. to 4 p.m. daily. Located on Route 235 in Northern Virginia. Call (703) 780-2000. There is an admission charge of $5. One of the most popular tourist spots in the country, you must visit Mount Vernon — the home of George Washington — during your visit to Virginia. Set on huge grounds, you can tour his house and see his original belongings, and you can even visit the site of his grave. You will never come closer to the Father of our country.

Museum of American Frontier Culture
Open year-round, every day. Located at 230 Frontier Drive in Staunton. Call (703) 332-7850. If you want to find out what it was really like in

the first days of America, then you should definitely visit this attraction. A perfect recreation of one of the oldest farms in America, you won't believe the hardships that our forefathers overcame to settle this land!

Museum and White House of the Confederacy

Open year-round, every day. Located at 1201 East Clay Street in Richmond. Call (804) 649-1861. One of the most historically significant buildings in America, this was the house where Jefferson Davis, the president of the Confederacy resided. The many beautiful antiques from the Civil War period will delight you, and you will be amazed to realize just how close this building is to the White House in Washington, D.C. — the capitols of the Confederate and United States of America were literally only a few miles apart!

Rising Sun Tavern

Open year-round, every day. Located at 1306 Caroline Street in Fredericksburg. Call (703) 371-1494. There is an admission charge of $5. Originally belonging to Charles Washington (George's brother), this tavern was a favorite hangout of all the famous revolutionaries! A truly intimate way to relive the history of our nation.

US Army Transportation Museum
Open year-round, 8 a.m. to 5 p.m. Monday to Friday, 10 a.m. to 5 p.m. Saturday. Located at the army base in Fort Eustis. Free. One of the best museums about military vehicles in the country, you are sure to love this attraction. You can see the different modes of transportation utilized by the American army during World War I and World War II, which will help you understand why these conflicts were fought in such different manners.

Virginia Discovery Museum
Open year-round, 9 a.m. to 5 p.m. daily. Located at 400 Ackley Lane in Charlottesville. Call (804) 293-5528. There is an admission charge of $5. A wonderful place to take your children for an afternoon; they will have a blast discovering more about the world around them. Attractions include a huge kaleidoscope that they can actually fit inside!

Historic Sites and Monuments

Arlington House
Open year-round, 9:30 a.m to 4:30 p.m. daily. Located in Arlington. Call (703) 557-0613. Free. Visit the house of one of the greatest military strategists of all time. Robert E. Lee resided here

prior to taking charge of Confederate forces in Virginia during the Civil War. His house, which is just feet from the famous Potomac river, is within the bounderies of Arlington National City.

Booker T. Washington National Monument

Open year-round, 8:30 a.m. to 5 p.m. daily. Located in Hardy. Call (703) 721-2094. There is an admission charge of $1 for each adult. This site commemorates the achievements of Booker T. Washington, the great African American leader, by preserving his boyhood home. Mr. Washington secretly taught himself how to read as a child.

George Washington Birthplace National Monument

Open year-round, 9 a.m. to 5 p.m. daily. Located off of Route 204 by the Potomac River, about 40 miles east of Fredricksburg. Call (804) 224-1732. There is an admission charge of $1 for each adult. This site commemorates the achievements of George Washington, general and the first president of the United States, by preserving the house in which he was born and raised. You can also see the cemetery where his family is buried.

US Marine Corps War Memorial

Always open. Located off of Route 50 in Arlington. Call (703) 285-2598. Free. Perhaps the most recognizable war memorial in the country, this sculpture captures the poses of Marines planting the American flag in Iwo Jima during World War II. This is truly a sight to behold.

National Parks and Recreation Areas

Appomattox Court House National Historical Park

Open year-round, 9 a.m. to 5 p.m. daily. Located just north of Appomattox, on Route 24. Call (804) 352-8987. There is an admission charge of $2 for each adult. One of the most important landmarks in American history, this is where the Union was officially saved when the Confederacy surrendered and ended the Civil War. This park is a wonderful place to spend a leisurely afternoon. There are no hiking trails or campsites, but you can have a nice picnic and bask in the sun. Moreover, soldiers lead discussions and presentations about this important event in United States history.

Great Falls Park

Open year-round, 7 a.m. to sunset daily. Located on Route 193 in Great Falls. Call (703) 285-2966. There is an admission charge of $3 for each vehicle. The spectacular view of the Great Falls from the Potomac River would make it worthwhile coming to this park, even if it didn't have so much more to offer. But it does have even more, such as many miles of trails, well suited to hikers at all levels of experience. You can also go fishing in the river, horseback riding through the fields, and picnicking at designated areas. In the winter, visitors enjoy the fine cross-country skiing that the park offers.

Prince William Forest Park

Open year-round, sunrise to sunset daily. Located on Route 619 in Triangle. Call (703) 221-7181. There is an admission charge of $3 for each vehicle (good for up to 7 days), and an additional charge of $7 for camping, collected nightly. This huge National Park preserves one of the most beautiful pine forests in the world. It is certainly an exhilarating place to visit! The forest is a haven for a wide variety of wildlife, so many nature lovers come equipped with cameras. The waters are rich in fish, so the fishing is great. There are almost 50 miles of hiking trails, well suited to all levels of experience. You can go camping in the designated campsites, or you can venture into the backcountry if you are more experienced.

Shenandoah National Park

Always open. Located on Route 211, just east of Luray. Call (703) 999-2243. There is a charge for camping. You've probably heard of this park from John Denver's famous song "Country Roads." The Blue Ridge Mountains which form one border of the park are a wonder to behold! There are over 500 miles of wooded hiking trails, well suited to all levels of experience. Many of the trails are also great for horseback riding. You can stop and have a picnic in several designated areas of the park, feasting on the beautiful scenery. In addition, you can camp overnight in one of the designated campsites, or you can go out into the backcountry if you prefer. There is even a lodge if you want to spend the night in a little bit more comfort.

Amusement Parks

Busch Gardens, The Old Country

Open from April to October, 10 a.m. to 10 p.m. daily (occasionally it extends its hours until midnight). Located on Route 60 in

Williamsburg. Call (804) 253-3350. There is an admission charge of $25, and an additional charge for parking. This *huge* amusement park celebrates the cultures of the various European countries from which our forefathers travelled to America. Its wonderful Medieval architecture is truly a sight to behold! It features almost 40 thrilling rides, such as fantasy simulators, several roller coasters, and a log ride. You can also meet some cute and cuddly animals in the petting zoo, and there are plenty of shows to watch. Some of the shows are gala events, utilizing animatronic puppets and trained animals, while others are personal performances staged by actors who roam around the park entertaining visitors. There are almost 50 restaurants where you can eat a variety of foods representative of the various cultures that the park commemorates.

King's Dominion
Open from March to October, 9 a.m. to 9 p.m. daily. Located on Route 30 in Doswell. Call (804) 876-5000. There is an admission charge of around $25, and an additional charge for parking. This amazing park features something for everyone. Like most large parks, it contains several different areas with rides in each that reflect a certain theme. There are almost 45 rides in all, 10 of which are designed specifi-

cally for younger children. Some of the more popular rides include several spine-tingling roller coasters, a carousel, a log ride, and a bobsled ride. There's also a huge replica of the Eiffel Tower, the top floor of which provides an amazing view. You can watch almost 15 different shows, featuring everything from actors in Hanna-Barbera costumes to lavish musical theatre productions. Famous singers occasionally perform concerts in the park, so don't forget to look into this. If you get hungry, you can eat at any of the almost 20 restaurants in the park, offering everything from snacks to full meals (I wouldn't leave the park without tasting some of its down-home country cookin'!).

TRAVEL GUIDE TO THE UNITED STATES

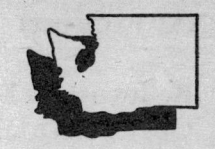

WASHINGTON

Attractions

Bellevue Art Museum
Open year-round, noon to 5 p.m. Tuesday to Sunday. Located at 10310 North East 4th Street in Bellevue. Call (206) 454-3322. Tuesdays are free. This museum features some of the finest art in the state.

New Dungeness Lighthouse
Open year-round, noon to 4 p.m. Saturday and Sunday. Located on Admiralty Island. This lighthouse, almost 130 years old and made almost entirely of brick, features truly magnificent architecture.

Pike Place Market
Open year-round, 9 a.m. to 5 p.m. daily. Located on Pike Street in Seattle. Call (206) 682-7453. Visit one of the oldest and best farmer's markets in the country! You can buy wonderful fruits, vegetables, sandwiches, meats, etc. (I'm getting hungry just writing this). A snack here sure makes a nice break from hotel food.

Seattle Center
Open year-round, daily. Located in northern Seattle. If you want to do some shopping, then this is the place to go in Seattle. This large center features hundreds of great stores (there's

even an amusement park, listed below). You'll also get to see the world famous Space Needle, where you can eat at a lovely restaurant and experience an incredible view.

State Capitol Museum
Open year-round, every day. Located at 211 West 21st Avenue in Olympia. This museum features exhibits on art, science, and local and natural history. The building itself is also beautiful.

Historic Sites and Monuments

Cape Disappointment Lighthouse
Open year-round, every day. Located 15 miles north of Astoria, by Fort Canby State Park. Free. The tallest lighthouse in Washington, it overlooks the "graveyard of the Pacific," where literally hundreds of ships have been wrecked.

Fort Vancouver National Historic Site
Open year-round, 9 a.m. to 5 p.m. daily. Located at 612 East Reserve Street in Vancouver. Call (206) 696-7655. $1 per adult or $3 for each family. This site was one of the major fur trading centers for the Hudson's Bay Company during the early 1800s. The United States Army also used it as a fort. Features tours and presentations.

San Juan Island National Historical Park

Open year-round, 9 a.m. to 6 p.m. daily. Located in Friday Harbor in Anacortes. Call (206) 378-2240. The park is free, but you will have to pay for transportation to the island. This island, once a central piece of land in a teritorial dispute between England and America, is now a symbol of peaceful relations. Although you cannot spend the night on the Island, it is a beautiful place to take a day trip. There are many miles of hiking trails that weave through British and American military forts. You can also have a lovely little picnic, and you can hear discussions and presentations about the history of the island.

Thomas Burke Memorial Washington State Museum

Open year-round, 9 a.m. to 4:30 p.m. Saturday and Sunday, and 11 a.m. to 5:30 p.m. Tuesday to Friday. Located on University of Washington in Seattle. Call (206) 543-5590. Free. This museum houses many items of historical significance, including Native American artifacts and cultural presentations from various Pacific Rim countries.

Whitman Mission National Historic Site

Open year-round, 8 a.m. to 4:30 p.m. daily. Located on Route 12, about 5 miles west of

Walla Walla. Call (509) 529-2761. $1 entry fee for each adult, or $3 for each vehicle. This mission, located on the Oregon Trail, was intended to convert the Cayuse Native Americans to Christianity. It features cultural exhibits and presentations.

National Parks and Recreation Areas

Coulee Dam National Recreation Area
Always open, and the climate is usually relatively mild during any season. Located at Coulee Dam. Call (509) 633-9441. Most of the campsites charge $7 each night. This recreation area is wonderful, whether you prefer aquatic sports or land activities. You can go boating or swimming in the lake, and you can go hiking and hunting in the woods around it. The campsites are well equipped with restrooms, picnic tables, and drinking water. A variety of boats, from small row boats to houseboats, can be rented. There are also several restaurants, and a few places where you can get food for your campsite.

Lake Chelan National Recreation Area
Always open, and the climate is usually relatively mild during any season. The recreation

area is accessible by boat from Chelan (it is possible to charter a boat every day from April to October; during other months you can only charter one every other day). Call (509) 682-2224 to charter a boat or for more information. Free. This beautiful recreation area is comprised of a valley and Lake Chelan, making for excellent trails and boating. Hiking is available at all skill levels, and the campsites have a variety of facilities (restrooms, picnic areas, restaurants). Some trails are smooth enough for bicycles, others are better suited to horses. If you want to experience nature with a bit more luxury, you can even stay at one of several lodges. There are plenty of Rangers to answer any questions you might have.

Mount Rainier National Park
Always open, but inclement weather often forces closure of certain areas in the winter. Located in Ashford. Call (206) 569-2211. There is an admission charge of $5 and an additional charge for camping. This national park contains a magnificent volcano (no longer active); at its base rest beautiful forests. The park is perfect for mountain climbing and hiking at all levels of experience. In the winter the cross-country skiing is excellent. Many animals populate the park, making it great for nature-watching. There are numerous campsites for you to spend

the night, or there are various lodges surrounding the park.

North Cascades National Park

Always open, but heavy snowfall frequently causes the park to close some areas in the winter. Located on Route 20 in Sedro Woolley. Call (206) 856-5700. There is an admission charge of $5 for each vehicle or $2 for each person, and an additional charge for camping. This national park features magnificent alpine terrain, including glaciers and mountain ranges. Hiking is exceptional; there are almost four hundred miles of trails, and you can also hike in the backcountry. There is also great fishing and boating on the lakes. There are plenty of campsites for you to spend the night, or you can make reservations to stay at a lodge.

Olympic National Park

Open year-round, 9 a.m. to 4 p.m. daily. Located in Port Angeles. Call (206) 452-4501. There is an admission charge from Memorial Day to Labor Day. If you thought you had to go to South America to see a rain forest, then you're wrong! Olympic National Park contains some of the most beautiful rain forests in the world, and they sit at the foot of gorgeous snow-capped mountains. The forests are perfect for hiking (there are many miles of trails), and you can also go mountain-biking or horseback riding. In the winter the park features excellent skiing, and in the summer you can have wonderful picnics. If you enjoy mountain climbing, then you won't be disappointed, and if you like camping, then you can stay in either designated camping areas or in the backcountry. You can even make reservations to spend the night in a lodge.

Amusement Parks

Riverfront Park

Open from March to October, daily. Located at North 507 Howard Street in Spokane. Call (509) 456-5512. Free admission, but there is a charge for each attraction. This huge amusement park is as noteworthy for its history as for its rides; one of the last World's Fairs was held there. There are almost 10 major rides, including a roller coaster, a carousel, and a flight simulator. You can also play mini-golf, watch an IMAX film, and attend several shows. You will also find plenty to eat within the park.

TRAVEL GUIDE TO THE UNITED STATES

WASHINGTON, D.C.

Attractions

Constitution Hall
Open year-round, 8:30 a.m. to 4 p.m. Monday to Friday, 1 p.m. to 5 p.m. Sunday. Located on 18th Street North West on Capitol Hill. Free. Not only does this building serve as the home to the Daughters of the American Revolution and the Decorative Arts Museum (featuring many beautiful historical items), but it also offers free performances and concerts on occasion. A really fun place to visit!

Folger Shakespeare Library
Open year-round, 10 a.m. to 4 p.m. Monday to Saturday. Located at 201 East Capitol Street South East on Capitol Hill. Free. Not only does this library house one of the best collections by and about William Shakespeare in the world, but it also has many works by other British authors. The architecture is quite magnificent, as it re-creates the look of Elizabethan England.

Library of Congress
Open year-round, every day. Located on Capitol Hill. Call (202) 707-5458. Free. Featuring almost 100 million books, this is the largest reference library in the world! If there is a subject that you would like to research, then this is the place to go (it is, for example, a haven

for genealogists). The building itself is quite beautiful, with tables made of mahogany.

National Geographic Society's Explorers Hall
Open year-round, every day. Located on 17th Street. Call (202) 857-7588. Free. One of the best interactive museums in the world, you will come out understanding more about our planet than you ever dreamed possible. Not only will you discover fascinating wonders of natural history, but you will also learn more about the different cultures across the globe!

The Smithsonian
Open year-round, every day. At various locations. Call (202) 357-2700. Free. Probably the greatest collection of museums in the entire world, you can see it all at the Smithsonian! There are museums of art, museums of history, museums of industry, and much, much more. The National Air and Space Museum, where you can view such pioneering aircrafts as The Spirit of Saint Louis, is the most popular museum on the planet! Don't forget to bring your camera, because this is a must-see!

Supreme Court
Open year-round, 9 a.m. to 5 p.m. weekdays. Located on 1st Street on Capitol Hill. Call (202)

479-3000. Free. One of the finest buildings in the city, this is the seat of justice and democracy in America. You can tour this fine structure, and learn all about the legal system in our country. Another must-see!

Union Station
Open year-round, every day. Located at 50 Massachusetts Avenue, North East on Capitol Hill. If you want to go shopping and sightseeing at the same time, then this is the place for you! Not only is it a breathtaking building (the inaugural ball even takes place here), but it also features some of the finest shops in the city.

Historic Sites and Monuments

Ford's Theatre National Historic Site
Open year-round, 9 a.m. to 5 p.m. daily. Located at 511 Tenth Street in Washington, D.C. Call (202) 426-6924. Free. This site commemorates the tragic events that led to the death of Abraham Lincoln, one of the finest presidents of the country. You can tour the Ford Theatre, where President Lincoln was shot by John Wilkes Booth, the house next door in which he was declared legally dead, and a museum highlighting his achievements. Despite the

solemn theme of the site, it is a surprisingly uplifting testament to the remarkable changes one man can bring about during his lifetime. Please note that, as the theater still houses performances, you should call first to confirm the hours of operation of the site.

Frederick Douglass Memorial
Open year-round, 9 a.m. to 4 p.m. daily. Located on W Street South East in Washington, D.C. Call (202) 426-5961. Free. This site commemorates the achievements of Frederick Douglass, a leader of the African American community during the late 1800s, by preserving the home in which he lived. He was also one of the first African Americans ever to hold a government position (foreign minister to Haiti). You can tour the house and watch presentations on Mr. Douglass' life. The house contains many of his personal belongings.

Lincoln Memorial
Open year-round, dawn to dusk daily. Located on 23rd Street North West in Washington, D.C. Call (202) 485-9880. Free. Housed within a huge building whose architecture is reminiscent of that of Classical Greece is the famous statue of a solemn-looking Abraham Lincoln seated in a grand chair. The walls are adorned with some of Mr. Lincoln's more famous and poetic words,

including his Second Inaugural Address ("A house divided...") and the Gettysburg Address ("Four score and seven years ago...").

Thomas Jefferson Memorial
Open year-round, 8 a.m. to midnight daily. Located on the Tidal Basin in Washington, D.C. Call (202) 485-9880. Free. This memorial commemorates the achievements of Thomas Jefferson, political theorist, and the country's 3rd president. Jefferson is considered by many to be one of the greatest statesmen who ever lived. The memorial features an impressive tower and a statue, and you can rent paddle boats to go in the Basin. There are also plenty of presentations about Mr. Jefferson to entertain and inform you.

Vietnam Veterans Memorial
Open year-round, every day. Located in West Potomac Park in Washington, D.C. Call (202) 485-9880. Free. The War in Vietnam is still one of the most controversial conflicts in which America has been involved. This memorial, which was not built until 15 years after the end of the War, honors the men and women who lost their lives in defense of Democracy. It bears the names of almost 60,000 American soldiers who died or are still listed as missing in action.

Washington Monument

Open year-round, 9 a.m. to 5 p.m. daily (from April to Labor Day, 8 a.m. to midnight). Located on the National Mall in Washington, D.C. Call (202) 485-9880. Free. One of the most famous landmarks in the country, this huge tower commemorates the achievements of George Washington, leader of the Revolutionary forces and first president of the United States of America. The view of the city from the observation level of the tower is quite magnificent!

The White House

Open year-round, 10 a.m. to noon Tuesday to Saturday. Located at 1600 Pennsylvania Avenue North West in Washington, D.C. Call (202) 755-7798. Free. Every president of the United States of America has lived in this famous house since its construction was completed in 1800 (George Washington personally chose its location). You can go on a marvelous tour of the facility, in which you can see portraits of many past presidents, precious antiques, and the beautiful architecture of the house itself. The tour is very popular, so you might have to get there as early as eight in the morning. Sometimes a ticket is needed, but not always, so call first. It is a fabulous thrill to know you are walking through the same corridors that presidents such as Lincoln, Roosevelt, and Kennedy walked through years ago!

TRAVEL GUIDE TO THE UNITED STATES

National Parks and Recreation Areas

Rock Creek Park

Open year-round, dawn to dusk daily, but certain attractions are closed at different times during the week. Located at 5200 Glover Road, North West in Washington, D.C. Call (202) 426-6832. There is a charge to rent horses and to use the golf course. This huge park in the middle of urban Washington, D.C. is the perfect place to spend the afternoon unwinding. There are many miles of hiking and horseback riding trails, well suited to all levels of experience (you can even get lessons in how to ride a horse). You can stop and have a picnic at any number of beautiful spots, and the grassy fields are perfect for leisurely strolls. You can even explore the universe in the planetarium.

Theodore Roosevelt Island

Open year-round, dawn to dusk daily. Located off the coast of Washington, D.C. (accessible on foot). Call (703) 285-2598. Free. This remote and secluded island is a lovely little haven to all sorts of wildlife. There are plenty of trails cutting through the thick woods, well suited to all levels of experience. The fishing is great, but you have to have a permit. If you like to watch for animals or birds, then don't forget to bring along your camera.

TRAVEL GUIDE TO THE UNITED STATES

WEST VIRGINIA

Attractions

Capitol Music Hall
Open year-round, every day. Located at 1015 Main Street in Wheeling. Call (800) 624-5456. If you love country music, then you won't want to miss this wonderful site! This is where the famous radio show *Jamboree USA* is recorded, and you might even get to see one of your favorite stars singing a song.

Cass Scenic Railroad Museum
Open from June to September, every day. Located in Cass. Call (304) 456-4300. There is an admission charge of $11 for adults and $5 for kids. Relive the dawn of one of the most glorious forms of transportation ever invented — the railroad! You can go on a wonderful train ride up Cheat Mountain in a locomotive that is almost 100 years old.

John Brown's Fort
Open year-round, 8 a.m. to 5 p.m. daily. Located in Old Arsenal Square in Harpers Ferry. Free. One of the most historically significant buildings in American history, you can visit the firehouse where army troops captured John Brown. Brown was an abolitionist, and he was highly active in the days prior to the Civil War.

National Radio Astronomy Observatory
Open at irregular times, so call first. Located in Green Banks. Call (304) 456-2011. Free. If you want to find out more about the universe around you, then take a fascinating tour of this facility! You will learn about the amazing procedures that scientists are undertaking to discover if life exists on other planets.

National Track and Field Hall of Fame
Open year-round, 9 a.m. to 4:30 p.m. weekdays, 9 a.m. to 5 p.m. Saturday, and noon to 5 p.m. Sunday. Located at 1524 Kanawha Boulevard East in Charleston. Call (304) 345-0087. Free. This museum commemorates great American track stars. Featured athletes include Jesse Owens and Carl Lewis. A must for sports fans.

Oglebay Park
Open year-round, every day. Located in Wheeling. Call (304) 242-3777. If you want to visit one place that has it all, then you should definitely come here! This huge and beautiful park features a planetarium, a zoo, a museum, and even a small ski resort in the winter. Prices and times for each attraction vary, so call first.

Historic Sites and Monuments

Grafton National Cemetery
Open year-round, 8 a.m. to 5 p.m. daily. Located at 431 Walnut Street in Grafton. Call (304) 265-2044. Free. This site is significant because it is the final resting place of T. Bailey Brown, the first Union soldier killed during the Civil War. A must see for war-history buffs.

West Virginia Independence Hall
Open year-round, 1 p.m. to 4 p.m. Sunday to Friday. Located on Market Street in Wheeling. Free. Celebrating the Independence of the United States, this structure used to be a customs house. Recently refurbished, it is now a museum in which you can see antiques and clothing from the 19th century.

National Parks and Recreation Areas

Harpers Ferry National Historical Park
Open year-round, 8 a.m. to 5 p.m. daily. Located in Harpers Ferry. Call (304) 535-6371, extension 6222. There is a charge for admission. One of the key spots during the Civil War, the Federal Armory contained within the park was

fought over bitterly by Union and Confederate forces. Control over the region changed virtually on a daily basis. The park is now a haven for fishing, hiking, and mountain climbing. There are many miles of beautiful and scenic trails, well suited to all levels of experience. The mountains are great, and the many streams and rivulets are rich in trout and other fish, but don't forget to get your permit before starting your ascent. There is no camping, but you can spend a wonderful afternoon eating a picnic lunch. You can also watch exciting re-creations of historical events, including John Brown's siege.

Amusement Parks

Camden Park

Open from April to October, 10 a.m. to 10 p.m. daily. Located on Route 60 West in Huntington. Call (304) 429-4231. You can either pay for each ride individually, or you can buy an unlimited ride pass for $10. If you want to reminisce about the good ol' days, then this park is definitely the place for you. It has retained its distinctive 1940s look, a style which truly makes one feel warm inside. It features almost 30 rides, about one-third of which are designed specifically for younger children. Some of the more popular rides include a carousel, several spectacular roller coasters, and a log ride. You can also go roller skating during the winter, or take a tour of the Ohio River in an old fashioned steamboat during the summer (this is a wonderful tour!). Famous country singers occasionally stop by to give concerts, so be sure to ask if anything is scheduled for the day you intend to visit. You can even visit a two thousand year old Native American burial chamber that happens to be on the park's grounds. There are almost 10 different restaurants where you can eat your fill, but the park is most famous for its southern-style cooking (you must not leave without trying the fried chicken). You can also bring your own food with you, if you prefer to do so.

TRAVEL GUIDE TO THE UNITED STATES

WISCONSIN

Attractions

Big Manitou Waterfall
Open year-round, every day. Located on Route 35 in Superior. There is a charge for admission. Visit the highest waterfall in the state of Wisconsin. The site is breathtaking and exhilarating.

Civil War Museum
Open year-round, 8 a.m. to 4 p.m. weekdays. Located at Lentz Hall in Kenosha (in Carthage College). Free. This is one of the finest museums in the country commemorating the Civil War. Features many items from that period.

Hawks Inn
Open year-round, every day. Located at 428 Wells Street in Delafield. Relive an important part of the history of the Old West. This inn was a popular resting point on the stagecoach route across this region of the country.

National Bowling Hall of Fame
Open year-round, 9 a.m. to 4 p.m. weekdays. Located at 5301 South 76th Street in Milwaukee. Call (414) 421-6400. Free. If you enjoy the sport of bowling, then this is a wonderful place to learn more about the pastime. As well as discovering more about some of the best bowlers

of all time, you will also find out about how the game was created.

State Capitol Building
Open year-round, 9 a.m. to 5 p.m. daily. Located in Capitol Park in Madison. Call (608) 266-0382. Free. Take a tour of this beautiful building, which features many exhibits of regional history.

Tallman House
Open year-round, every day. Located at 440 North Jackson Street in Janesville. Tour the 150 year old house once owned by William M. Tallman, an abolitionist who played an important role in the Underground Railroad of fugitive slaves. The house has been completely refurbished, and it now houses many historical exhibits.

Waelderhaus
Open year-round, every day, with tours at 2 p.m., 3 p.m., and 4 p.m.. Located on West Riverside Drive in Kohler. Free. Tour the headquarters of the Girl Scouts of America. This fascinating center includes such exhibits as the Girl Scout Laws carved into large pieces of wood. This is a really exciting way to find out more about an organization that has truly become a part of American culture.

Washburn Observatory
Open from May to October, 9 p.m. to 11 p.m. on the 1st and 3rd Wednesday of each month. Located on Observatory Drive in the University of Wisconsin in Madison. Free. The scientists at this observatory will let you look through their giant telescope at the stars above.

Historic Sites and Monuments

Cushing Memorial State Park
Open year-round, dawn to dusk daily. Located in Delafield. Free. This park, which is in honor of three brothers who fought in the Civil War, is a wonderful place to spend an afternoon.

G.A.R. Memorial Hall Museum
Open year-round, 9 a.m. to 4:30 p.m. weekdays (9 a.m. to 4:30 p.m. daily from Memorial Day to November). Located in the Capital Building in Madison. Free. This museum will take you on a fascinating tour of the histories of the Civil War and the Spanish-American War. There are many wonderful displays and items, including costumes, maps, plans, and weapons.

Peshtigo Fire Museum and Monument
Open from Memorial Day to October, every day. Located on Oconto Avenue in Peshtigo.

Free, but donations are requested. This museum commemorates the valor of those who fought the most devastating forest fire ever to occur in this country. There were over one thousand deaths as a result of the fire.

National Parks and Recreation Areas

Apostle Islands National Lakeshore
Open year-round, 8 a.m. to 4:30 p.m. daily from Labor Day to October, 8 a.m. to 4:30 p.m. Monday to Friday from November to Memorial Day, and 8 a.m. to 6 p.m. daily from Memorial Day to Labor Day; severe weather often forces closure during the winter. Located on Route 13 in Bayfield. Call (715) 779-3397. Free, except for the cost of chartering a boat. Including more than 20 islands which feature dramatic cliffs and beautiful woods, this lakeshore is an impressive sight. It is well suited to boating, swimming, scuba diving, hiking, and camping. There are hundreds of miles of hiking trails through the various islands, for all levels of experience. There are plenty of campsites on the islands. You can also camp and hike in the backcountry. You can even tour many historic sites, such as old lighthouses.

Saint Croix National Scenic Riverway

Open year-round, every day, but many attractions close during the winter. Located in Saint Croix Falls. Call (715) 483-3284. Free. This riverway is naturally suited to water-lovers: you can boat, swim, and fish. You can also camp and hike, and in the winter you can go cross-country skiing. There are many campsites available, but there are no cabins or lodges. You can bring your own food to many picnic sites, but there are no restaurants.

Amusement Parks

Riverview Park

Open from May to October, 9 a.m. to 11 p.m. daily. Located on Highway 12, a few miles south of Highway 13, in Wisconsin Dells. Call (608) 254-2608. You can either pay $15 for an unlimited ride pass, or you can pay for each ride separately; there is no charge for parking. This lovely park features over 45 rides on its attractive grounds, almost half of which are water rides. Some of the more popular ones include go-karts and spinning amusement rides. You can also visit a petting zoo, watch a magician, and go on a guided tour of the beautiful woods.

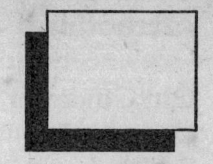

WYOMING

Attractions

Old Governor's Mansion
Open year-round, 9 a.m. to 5 p.m. Monday to Friday. Located at 300 East 21st Street in Cheyenne. Call (307) 777-7878. Free. This gorgeous mansion housed the state's governors until the mid 1970s. View historic furniture and tour the grounds.

State Capitol
Open year-round, 8:30 a.m. to 5 p.m. Monday to Friday. Located on Capitol Avenue in Cheyenne. Call (307) 777-7220. Free. This beautiful capitol building features a humongous dome made of gold. It also has many examples of Southwestern art on display.

Wind River Indian Reservation
Open year-round, dawn to dusk daily. Located in Fort Washakie. Populated almost entirely by the Shoshone tribe of Native Americans, this reservation features many interesting sights.

Historic Sites and Monuments

Buffalo Bill Historical Center
Open year-round, every day. Located at 720 Sheridan Avenue in Cody. This center houses

four museums chronicling the history of Wyoming. Exhibits include Southwestern Art, Winchester rifles, and Buffalo Bill's house.

Devils Tower National Monument
Open year-round, every day. Located off Route 24 in Devils Tower. Call (307) 467-5370. $1 per person or $3 for each vehicle. This monument has been seen in countless movies and TV shows, such as *Close Encounters of the Third Kind*. It is a natural wonder, climbing over 860 feet to its perfectly flat top. Beautiful landscape, perfect for photography, mountain climbing, or hiking.

Fossil Butte National Monument
Open year-round, 8 a.m. to 4:30 p.m. daily (8 a.m. to 7 p.m. during the summer). Located 14 miles west of Kemmerer. Call (307) 877-4455. Free. This national monument is brimming with fossils of fish that are 50 million years old. Beautiful for hiking and examining fossils.

National Parks and Recreation Areas

Grand Teton National Park
Always open. Located on Route 26 in Moose. Call (307) 733-2880. There is a charge of $5-$10

if you want to bring your boat with you. A haven for some of the most beautiful wild animals in the country, this National Park features cool lakes and stunning mountains. There are over two hundred miles of trails for you to hike on, well suited to all levels of experience. The mountian climbing is great, and the abundant snowfall during the winter months is perfect for cross-country skiing. You can camp in either designated campsites or in the backcountry, or you can rent a lodge if you want a bit more comfort (don't forget to make reservations).

Yellowstone National Park
Always open, but many campsites close during the winter months due to inclement weather. Located on Route 20. Call (307) 344-7381. There is an admission charge of $10 for each vehicle (but the permit is good for seven days) or $4 for each individual; and there is an additional charge of up to $10 for camping. The largest and the oldest of America's national parks, Yellowstone is famous for its *thousands* of geysers. You can do just about anything here—hiking, boating, cross-country skiing, swimming, stagecoach riding, horseback riding, fishing, etc. There are over one thousand miles of hiking trails! Plenty of campsites, lodges and cabins are available.